The Most D Breakfast Ideas for Everyone

Breakfast Cookbook for A Great Start of The Day

BY: Valeria Ray

License Notes

Copyright © 2019 Valeria Ray All Rights Reserved

All rights to the content of this book are reserved by the Author without exception unless permission is given stating otherwise.

The Author have no claims as to the authenticity of the content and the Reader bears all responsibility and risk when following the content. The Author is not liable for any reparations, damages, accidents, injuries or other incidents occurring from the Reader following all or part of this publication.

A Special Reward for Purchasing My Book!

Thank you, cherished reader, for purchasing my book and taking the time to read it. As a special reward for your decision, I would like to offer a gift of free and discounted books directly to your inbox. All you need to do is fill in the box below with your email address and name to start getting amazing offers in the comfort of your own home. You will never miss an offer because a reminder will be sent to you. Never miss a deal and get great deals without having to leave the house! Subscribe now and start saving!

https://valeria-ray.gr8.com

Contents

Perfect Breakfast Recipes 6

(1) Quinoa and Fresh Fruits 7

(2) Tater Tots Casserole 9

(3) French Toasts Topped with Berries 12

(4) Breakfast Lasagna 15

(5) Chia Seed Smoothie 18

(6) Mexican Crepes 20

(7) Banana and Chocolate Chip Bread 24

(8) Lemon Cake 27

(9) Eggy Biscuits 31

(10) Baked Hash Browns 34

(11) Glazed Donuts 37

(12) Sweet Potato Tortillas 41

(13) Spicy Peach Tasty Smoothie 44

(14) Egg and Cheese Biscuit Sandwich 47

(15) Potato and Vegetable Casserole 50

(16) Wonderful Peach Cobbler for Breakfast 53

(17) Banana Pancakes 56

(18) Sour Cream, Chives and Eggs Muffins 59

(19) English Muffin Breakfast Pizza 62

(20) Chocolate and Strawberry Parfait 65

(21) Benedict Crepes 68

(22) Fruit and Pistachios Shake 71

(23) Coffee Muffins 74

(24) Blueberries and French Toasts Casserole 77

(25) Avocado and Apple Salad 80

About the Author 83

Author's Afterthoughts 85

Perfect Breakfast Recipes

(1) Quinoa and Fresh Fruits

I love quinoa and make a point to make it at least a few times per week. It might be an acquired taste for some of you, so use a grain of your choice. You can also add your own favorite sweet toppings. In this case, we will add berries, yogurt and a few other essentials.

List of Ingredients:

- 2 cups cooked quinoa of your choice
- Pinch cinnamon
- 2 cups fresh berries of your choice (strawberries, raspberries, blackberries, blueberries)
- 1 cup Greek plain yogurt
- 2 Tablespoons flaxseeds

Yield: 4

Cooking Time: 40 minutes

MMMMMMMMMMMMMMMMMMMMMMMMMMMM

Procedure:

In tow bowls, divide the quinoa and yogurt.

Stir to combine and add the berries, flax seeds and cinnamon on top of each quinoa mixture.

Enjoy!

(2) Tater Tots Casserole

My children love tater tots. I don't blame them, I also loved them as a kid. They are like an upgraded version of French fries mixed with hash browns. They are easy to use in a casserole. Let's make sure we add some flavors, some spices and in this case bacon to make it tasty.

List of Ingredients:

- 1 package of tater tots
- 6 slices turkey bacon
- 1 cup sour cream
- 2 tablespoons fresh minced chives
- 2 Tablespoons fresh minced parsley
- 4 large eggs
- 1 tablespoon chili powder
- ½ teaspoons onion powder
- ½ teaspoons garlic powder
- Salt, black pepper
- 1 cup whole milk

Yield: 4-6

Cooking Time: 50 minutes

MMMMMMMMMMMMMMMMMMMMMMMMMMM

Procedure:

Preheat the oven to 400 degrees F.

Get the tater tots out of the freezer 30 minutes ahead.

Grease a large baking dish and set aside.

Cook the bacon in the microwave for about 5 minutes. It should be almost cook perfectly. Crumble and set aside.

In a mixing bowl, combine the sour cream, milk, eggs, fresh herbs and all spices.

Place the tater tots with the sour cream sauce and the bacon and stir so all is well combined.

Place in the oven for about 40 minutes.

Enjoy any morning.

(3) French Toasts Topped with Berries

I have to say I prefer French toast to pancakes. I grew up in a French toast house. My mother would religiously cook some French toast almost every weekend morning. I remember smelling them form the living room as I was watching my Saturday morning cartoons. This recipe will propose different toppings, but same delicious French toasts recipe.

List of Ingredients:

French toasts

- 4 thick slices of bread (sourdough or Italian)
- 2 large eggs
- 3 Tablespoons whole milk
- Pinch cinnamon
- ½ teaspoons vanilla extract
- Butter for cooking

Topping

- 1 cup fresh raspberries
- 1 cup fresh blueberry
- 4 Tablespoons white sugar
- ¼ cup orange juice

Yield: 4

Cooking Time: 30 minutes

MMMMMMMMMMMMMMMMMMMMMMMMMMM

Procedure:

In a mixing bowl, whisk the eggs with the milk, vanilla, cinnamon.

Then, heat some butter in a large frying pan.

If you can fit all 4 slices of bread at the same time, go for it.

If not, do what you can.

Dip one slice ta a time in the egg mixture, make sure it's not dropping and put in the pan.

Cook about 3 minutes on each side.

Meanwhile, in a small saucepan, heat the berries, white sugar and orange juice until all the sugar is melted.

When serving, place one French toast with generous portion of the berries mixture.

(4) Breakfast Lasagna

Now this is a very unique recipe. Serving lasagna for breakfast does not sound right at first. However, when you realize that it is made with various breakfast ingredients, then you understand that it does make a lot of sense after all. Make sure you use your favorite meat, either sausage, bacon or oven smoked ham.

List of Ingredients:

- 1 box precooked lasagna noodles
- 1 pound crumbled Italian sausage
- 3 cups fresh baby spinach leaves
- 1 tablespoon minced garlic
- Salt, black pepper
- ½ teaspoons dried cumin
- 2 cups ricotta cheese
- ½ cup whole milk
- 6 large eggs
- 1 cup shredded Mozzarella cheese

Yield: 4-6

Cooking Time: 60 minutes

MMMMMMMMMMMMMMMMMMMMMMMMMMMM

Procedure:

Preheat the oven to 375 F.

Then grease a large rectangle baking dish and set aside.

In a medium pan, cook the Italian sausage with the minced garlic for about 15 minutes, or until done. Add the baby spinach to the mixture for last few minutes of cooking.

In a mixing bowl, combine the ricotta cheese, eggs and milk. Add the cumin, salt, pepper.

Assemble your lasagna as followed: bottom layer of noodles, next a layer of meat and spinach, following by cheese mixture. Repeat until another time and make sure you end with a layer of noodles.

Sprinkle the Mozzarella cheese on top and bake in the oven for about 45-60 minutes.

Serve with pride on a Saturday morning.

(5) Chia Seed Smoothie

Let's finish this cookbook with a very healthy recipe, once more. Using chia seeds can add so many nutrients in your daily life. Chia seeds provide you antioxidants, proteins and fibers. So, no need to fill up with meat in the morning. Sprinkle some chia seeds in your recipe and you're good to go!

List of Ingredients:

- 1 cup unsweetened cashew milk
- 1 cup soy milk
- ½ teaspoons almond extract
- 3 Tablespoons chia seeds
- 1 large ripped banana
- 1 tablespoon agave syrup
- 1 cup fresh berries of your choice

Yield: 2

Cooking Time: 15 minutes

MMMMMMMMMMMMMMMMMMMMMMMMMMMM

Procedure:

Place the cashew milk in blender with the chia seeds. Let it rest for 5 minutes.

Slice the banana and add to the blender, as well as the soy milk, agave syrup, berries and almond extract.

Activate and once the mixture is nice and smooth pour into 2 tall glasses.

(6) Mexican Crepes

I am sure you have had crepes before. But I am pretty sure you never had a crepe including some Mexican ingredients. This is going to be fun and yummy. Crepes are thin, so make sure you finely dice the ingredients, so they do not become too heavy for the crepe.

List of Ingredients:

Crepes

- 1 cup all-purpose flour
- 2 eggs
- ½ cup soy milk
- 2 Tablespoons unsalted butter
- Pinch salt
- ½ teaspoons baking powder

Sauce

- 1 medium can diced tomatoes
- 1 tablespoon tomato paste
- 1 tablespoon green chilies
- ½ teaspoons cayenne pepper
- 1 tablespoon olive oil
- ½ chopped yellow onion
- 1 can seasoned black beans

Toppings

- 1 cup shredded Monterey jack cheese
- Sour cream
- Chopped fresh cilantro

Yield: 4

Cooking Time: 40 minutes

Procedure:

Making crepes is a lot like making pancakes, except that you want the result to be much thinner.

Prepare the crepes batter. In a mixing bowl, combine the flour salt and baking powder. Add the eggs, soy milk and melted butter.

Stir until you are satisfied with the consistency, if it's too thick, add a little milk.

Heat some butte in a medium frying pan and pour the mixture for one crepe at a time.

Meanwhile, in a medium saucepan, you can combine the ingredients for the sauce. Start by sautéed the onions in olive oil first and add all the other ingredients listed under sauce. Keep the sauce simmering until all crepes are ready.

When ready to plate, fill the crepe with generous portion of the sauce, and add some cheese also inside.

Fold the crepe and add a touch of sour cream and sprinkle some fresh cilantro.

Get ready to eat while it's warm.

(7) Banana and Chocolate Chip Bread

The combination of fresh mashed bananas with sweet chocolate chips never fails to satisfy. You could add some nuts as well, but I prefer to keep it just chocolate and bananas. Sometimes I will make a different variation, made with only bananas and walnuts.

List of Ingredients:

- 2 large ripped bananas
- 1 cup brown sugar
- ½ cup unsalted butter (room temperature)
- 2 medium eggs
- 1 cup tapioca flour
- 1 cup all-purpose flour
- ¾ cup rice flour
- ½ cup sour cream
- 1 teaspoon vanilla extract
- 1 teaspoon baking powder
- 1 cup semi-sweet chocolate chips

Yield: 4-6

Cooking Time: 60 minutes

MMMMMMMMMMMMMMMMMMMMMMMMMMMMMM

Procedure:

Preheat the oven to 375 degrees F.

Grease a loaf pan and then set aside.

In a large mixing bowl, combine the flours, baking powder, brown sugar.

In a second bowl, combine the vanilla, sour cream, mashed bananas, butter.

Then, combine both mixtures in the biggest bowl.

Add the chocolate chips, stir again and pour the mixture into the pan.

Bake for 50 minutes or until a knife comes out clean from cutting the center.

(8) Lemon Cake

What a great way to start your day. A piece of this lemon cake, a warm tea and maybe reading the newspaper on your terrace, in peace. Of course, the cake would be as good if you have to pack it to go and munch on it in your car on your way to work. However, I like to think that you will take your time savoring it when you can.

List of Ingredients:

Topping

- 1 cup all-purpose flour
- ¼ cup coconut oil (room temperature)
- 1/3 cup brown sugar
- 1 tablespoon lemon juice
- 1 tablespoon orange juice
- 1 tablespoon lemon zest

Cake

- 2 cups all-purpose flour
- 1 tablespoon baking powder
- 1 teaspoon baking soda
- ½ teaspoons salt
- 1 tablespoon zest lemon
- 3 Tablespoons lemon juice
- ½ cup coconut oil (room temperature)
- 2 small eggs
- 1 teaspoon vanilla extract
- ¾ cup brown sugar
- ½ cup whole milk

Yield: 4-6

Cooking Time: 55 minutes

MMMMMMMMMMMMMMMMMMMMMMMMMMMMM

Procedure:

Preheat the oven to 350 degrees F.

Spray with coconut oil; a large round cake pan.

In a mixing bowl, combine the dry Ingredients: four, baking powder baking soda, salt and brown sugar.

In a different bowl, combine the lemon zest, lemon juice, coconut oil, eggs, vanilla and milk.

Add the wet mixture to the dry one and stir until no more lumps.

Dump into the baking dish.

Prepare the topping next.

In a bowl, simply mix all ingredients., and add on top of the cake.

Bake everything for 50 minutes.

(9) Eggy Biscuits

This is a fun way to serve your eggs in the morning. You combine the delicious golden biscuits with whole sunny side up eggs. It is up to you if you want to add meat. I certainly recommend it if you are planning this breakfast item to hold you up for several hours.

List of Ingredients:

- 4 large eggs
- Fresh minced parsley
- Salt, black pepper
- Smoked paprika
- Biscuits batter
- 2 cups all-purpose flour
- 1 cup low fat sour cream
- ½ teaspoons salt
- 1 tablespoon white sugar
- ¼ cup unsalted butter (room temperature)
- 1 teaspoon baking powder
- 1 cup shredded sharp Cheddar cheese

Yield: 4

Cooking Time: 50 minutes

MMMMMMMMMMMMMMMMMMMMMMMMMMMM

Procedure:

Preheat the oven to 350 degrees F.

Grease a baking sheet and set aside for now.

In a mixing bowl, combine the flour sugar, baking powder, salt and cheese.

Add the sour cream and butter and stir until the biscuit batter seems of the perfect consistency and without lumps.

Place generous portion of the batter, large circles on the baking sheet.

You should make 4 large ones.

Make a whole in the middle of each one and crack an egg in each hole.

Season egg with salt, pepper and smoke paprika.

Place in the oven to bake for 30 minutes or until you are certain the eggs and biscuits are done.

Enjoy with ketchup if you wish.

(10) Baked Hash Browns

Casseroles are awesome. You can also choose to make this one in your slow cooker and bring it at work for breakfast potluck. I prefer to use the oven when I can however, it makes it a little crunchy on top. I have tried to add many different types of cheeses, meat and veggies, and the recipe below transcribes my favorite outcome.

List of Ingredients:

- 1 package of frozen hash browns or 5 shredded white potatoes (peeled)
- 1 cup sour cream
- 1 cup ricotta cheese
- 1 cup shredded Swiss cheese
- 2 cups sliced fresh button mushrooms
- 1 can cream of mushrooms
- ¼ cup whole milk
- 1 tablespoon minced garlic
- 1 small diced sweet onion
- 1 teaspoon cumin
- Salt, black pepper

Yield: 4-6

Cooking Time: 55 minutes

MMMMMMMMMMMMMMMMMMMMMMMMMMMM

Procedure:

Preheat the oven to 400 degrees F.

No need to thaw the hash browns ahead.

In a small pan, sautéed the mushrooms with garlic and onions for 10 minutes, in little olive oil.

Set aside in a large mixing bowl.

You will add the cream of mushrooms, milk, sour cream, ricotta cheese and seasonings and mix altogether.

Dump into a large baking dish and dump the hash browns.

Combine very well with wooden spoon and then top off the casserole with Swiss cheese.

Bake for 50 minutes.

(11) Glazed Donuts

Donuts are a classic breakfast time staple and you can make them anytime during the year, the kids and adults will be equally delighted. If you love the glazed donuts you can buy at the store, you will definitely be excited about tasting this homemade version of them.

List of Ingredients:

- Coconut oil for frying
- 3 cups tapioca flour
- 1 cup all-purpose flour
- ¾ cup white sugar
- ¼ cup brown sugar
- 1 teaspoon baking powder
- Pinch salt
- ½ teaspoons Ground nutmeg
- ½ teaspoons Ground cinnamon
- 2 large eggs
- 1/3 cup Greek yogurt
- ½ cup pumpkin puree
- 2 Tablespoons coconut oil
- ½ teaspoons vanilla extract

Glaze

- 2 ½ cups confectioners' sugar
- ½ teaspoons vanilla extract
- ½ cup coconut milk

Yield: 4-6

Cooking Time: 40- minutes

MMMMMMMMMMMMMMMMMMMMMMMMMMMMM

Procedure:

If you are using a deep frying, make sure you place the coconut oil and start heating it.

If not a thick and deep saucepan will do and start heating up the oil as well.

In a mixing bowl, combine the dry ingredients for the batter: flours, sugars, baking powder, salt, spices.

In a second bowl, combine the eggs, yogurt, pumpkin puree, oil and vanilla extract.

Then, pour the wet mixture in the dry one and combine well.

From your donuts and drop them in hot oil when ready.

Meanwhile, prepare the glaze in a small pan, combine the milk, confectioner's sugar and vanilla. Stir until all melted without lumps.

Let the glaze cool down so you can apply it easier.

When the donuts are ready, place them on paper towels to let them the excess oil absorbed.

Glaze them when they are cool and enjoy one bite at a time!

(12) Sweet Potato Tortillas

Here is one brilliant idea among the many brilliant recipes we could have chosen. Tortilla shells can hold almost anything you want. For this recipe you will be serving sweet potato with egg and maple syrup. Let's get cooking!

List of Ingredients:

- Soft tortilla breads
- First idea
- 1 shredded sweet potato
- 2 eggs
- 1 tablespoon coconut oil
- 1 tablespoon maple syrup
- Pinch cinnamon

Yield: 2

Cooking Time: 30 minutes

MMMMMMMMMMMMMMMMMMMMMMMMMMMM

Procedure:

Cook the sweet potato for 5 minutes on high temperature in the microwave.

Peel and shred the potato. Place it in a bowl.

Mix in the other ingredients, except the oil.

Heat the coconut oil and cook all together the eggs, potatoes and maple syrup until the eggs are done.

Fix you tortillas by filling them with this delicious combination.

(13) Spicy Peach Tasty Smoothie

Simple in the morning often works best. Preparing a smoothie is relatively simple and will hold you up until lunch. For this recipe, make sure you use fresh peaches, it will be much better. Also, don't over spice it. Add just a little so you don't overpower the natural delicious taste, or more if needed.

List of Ingredients:

- 2 large fresh peaches
- 1 tablespoon maple syrup
- ½ teaspoons vanilla extract
- Pinch ground ginger
- 1 cup coconut milk
- 1 cup Greek plain yogurt

Yield: 2

Cooking Time: 10 minutes

MMMMMMMMMMMMMMMMMMMMMMMMMMMM

Procedure:

Clean and peel the peaches. Slice them in pieces as well.

Place the peaches in your high-speed blender's container.

Add the yogurt, coconut milk, ginger, vanilla and maple syrup.

Activate for a few minutes or until the consistency is perfectly smooth.

Taste and adjust the spices or ample syrup as needed.

Pour into 2 glasses and enjoy for breakfast.

(14) Egg and Cheese Biscuit Sandwich

This recipe is not supposed to be the diet type. It is supposed to be filling to keep you going until lunch time! Sure, you can always modify it and use low fat Feta cheese and no bacon, but that's the point? I certainly am proud this serve this refined and high calories breakfast to my husband and his brother before they leave on a fishing trip.

List of Ingredients:

- Biscuits batter
- 2 cups all-purpose flour
- 1 teaspoon baking powder
- 1 tablespoon brown sugar
- Pinch salt
- 6 Tablespoons coconut oil (room temperature)
- 3-4 cup sour cream

Filing

- 4 slices ham
- ½ cup crumbled blue cheese
- 1 cup baby spinach leaves
- Salt, black pepper
- 1 tablespoon hot sauce

Yield: 4

Cooking Time: 40 minutes

MMMMMMMMMMMMMMMMMMMMMMMMMMMM

Procedure:

Preheat the oven to 350 degrees F.

Prepare the biscuits from scratch. Mix into a large bowl the dry ingredients and add the coconut oil and sour cream.

Place 4 large biscuits on a greased baking sheet and bake for 20 minutes.

Meanwhile, get the other ingredients ready.

Once the biscuit comes out, let them cool down for a minute and cut in middle, add ham, blue cheese, spinach and seasonings.

Place back in the oven for 5 minutes and enjoy next.

(15) Potato and Vegetable Casserole

I used to love going out for breakfast with my parents, just so I could order a side of roasted breakfast potatoes. Now, I love making them for my children. This casserole adds a little more than potatoes and it's my way to tell my children how much I love them (also sneaking in some veggies in it).

List of Ingredients:

- 3 cups diced red potatoes
- 1 diced red bell pepper
- 1 diced green bell pepper
- 1 tablespoon minced garlic
- 1 medium diced red onion
- 2 Tablespoons olive oil
- ¼ cup sliced black olives
- 1 tablespoon Cajun spices
- Salt, black pepper

Yield: 3-4

Cooking Time: 45 minutes

MMMMMMMMMMMMMMMMMMMMMMMMMMM

Procedure:

I tend to microwave the potatoes ahead, this is simply to reduce the time spent cooking them in the pan. You could also blanche them in boiling water, it's your choice. You do want to only pre-cook them, so they are not mushy.

Dice the potatoes. I choose to keep the skin on, it has more nutrients that way.

In a large frying pan, heat the olive oil and place the bell peppers, garlic and onion to cook for 10 minutes.

Add the potatoes, the spices and the black olives. Stir and keep cooking on medium-low temperature for about 20 minutes.

Serve with eggs or as is with a side of sour cream.

(16) Wonderful Peach Cobbler for Breakfast

A cobbler might sound more like a dessert than a breakfast to some of you? However, if you use breakfast ingredients to create it, then it becomes a breakfast, doesn't it? Use fresh peaches to begin with, it will make a big difference. I also like to emphasize on the flaxseeds and your choice of coconut or almond flour.

List of Ingredients:

- 5-6 medium fresh peaches
- ½ cup water
- ¼ cup orange juice
- 1 teaspoon cinnamon
- ¼ cup brown sugar

Topping

- 1 cup rolled oats
- ¾ cup coconut flour
- ¼ cup brown sugar
- 3 tablespoons unsalted butter
- ½ cup baking powder
- ½ baking soda
- ½ cup whole milk

Yield: 4-6

Cooking Time: 55 minutes

Procedure:

Preheat the oven to 350 degrees F.

Peel and slice the fresh peaches.

Place them in a saucepan with the water, orange juice, cinnamon and brown sugar.

Keep on low temperature until the sugar has melted.

Dump into a square baking dish you previously greased.

Prepare the topping by mixing into bowl the baking soda, baking powder, oats, coconut flour, and brown sugar.

Melt the melt and add to the mixture.

It will be crumbly, just how we like the topping for a cobbler.

Sprinkle on top of the peaches mixture and bake in the oven for 45 minutes.

Enjoy for breakfast with some plain yogurt.

(17) Banana Pancakes

Bananas and pancakes seem like a great combination. You might wonder if we mean that we put bananas in our pancake mix or simply add sliced bananas on top of them. As a matter of fact, we choose to do both. what can I say, we are bananas lovers!

List of Ingredients:

- 1 ½ cups almond flour
- 2 medium eggs
- 3 Tablespoons brown sugar
- 1 teaspoon baking powder
- 1 teaspoon kosher salt
- ½ cup buttermilk
- ¼ cup almond milk
- 1 teaspoon almond extract
- 1 teaspoon orange zest
- 2 large bananas
- Maple syrup or honey

Yield: 3-4

Cooking Time: 30 minutes

MMMMMMMMMMMMMMMMMMMMMMMMMMMM

Procedure:

In a first mixing bowl, combine the dry ingredients: almond four, brown sugar, baking powder, salt.

In the second one, combine the wet ones: almond milk, buttermilk, almond extract, orange zest, 1 mashed banana and eggs.

Combine both mixture together and stir.

Heat some butter or coconut oil, your preference in a medium frying pan.

Cook the pancakes as you normally do.

Add some sliced bananas on the pancakes and syrup or honey as you wish.

(18) Sour Cream, Chives and Eggs Muffins

These cute eggs muffins are popular with kids. Have you noticed how much kids love the sour cream and chives potato chips? Then, it's time to give them that flavor in a healthier alternative. I love how the kids now grab one on their way to school or ask me to make them for after-school snacks.

List of Ingredients:

- 8 large eggs
- 1 cup whole milk
- 1 cup sour cream
- ½ cup all-purpose flour
- 3 tablespoons minced fresh chives
- 1 teaspoon cayenne pepper
- Salt, black pepper

Yield: 6

Cooking Time: 45 minutes

MMMMMMMMMMMMMMMMMMMMMMMMMMMM

Procedure:

Preheat the oven to 375 degrees F.

Grease a muffin tin pan and set aside.

In a large mixing bowl, combine the eggs, milk, sour cream, spices and herbs.

Then, gradually add the flour and stir constantly.

Pour the mixture into the muffin tin holes and bake in the oven for 40 minutes.

Enjoy with a little hot sauce if you like.

(19) English Muffin Breakfast Pizza

I have eaten pizza in the morning many times in my adult life. However, usually it's because we have left over from the pizza, we ordered the night before and we are still too tired to cook anything else. This time, we will be cooking these mini pizzas from scratch.

List of Ingredients:

- 4 English muffins
- 4 Tablespoons marinara sauce
- 1 cup shredded Mozzarella cheese
- 1 cup chopped pepperoni
- 1 tablespoon minced parsley

Yield: 4

Cooking Time: 40 minutes

MMMMMMMMMMMMMMMMMMMMMMMMMMMM

Procedure:

Preheat the oven to 400 degrees F.

Grease a baking sheet and set aside.

Pull apart he English muffins, so you have 8 pieces total and place them on the baking sheet.

Spread the marinara Maiandra sauce on each of them.

Add the chopped pepperoni and the cheese.

Place in the oven for 20 minutes or until the cheese is completely melted.

Serve the breakfast pizza hot and decorate with fresh parsley if you like.

(20) Chocolate and Strawberry Parfait

This breakfast is so beautiful and appetizing. If you tend to skip breakfast, this might just help you break that bad habit. When I make it for my husband, he looks at me as if it was our anniversary or some other special occasion?

List of Ingredients:

- 1 tablespoon Cacao powder
- 3 cups Greek yogurt, plain
- 1 tablespoon flaxseeds
- Pinch cinnamon
- 2 cups sliced fresh strawberries
- 1 tablespoon white sugar

Yield: 2

Cooking Time: 20 minutes

MMMMMMMMMMMMMMMMMMMMMMMMMM

Procedure:

No one said you can't have a little touch of chocolate in the morning.

In a bowl, combine the yogurt, cacao powder, cinnamon and sugar.

Wash and slice the fresh strawberries and set aside.

Get ready to assemble in your favorite dessert cups or a clear mug.

Use a layer of the yogurt, a layer of slices strawberries, some flaxseeds and repeat.

Enjoy slowly!

(21) Benedict Crepes

If you have tasted eggs Benedict before, you know that they must include some hollandaise sauce, rich creamy sauce and smoked ham. It will usually be served on a bagel or English muffin but this time we decoded to serve it on or in a crepe instead.

List of Ingredients:

- 1 ½ cup all-purpose flour
- 1 teaspoon baking powder
- 2 large eggs
- ½ cup sour cream
- 1 tablespoon minced fresh minced parsley
- 1 tablespoon minced fresh chives
- Pinch salt
- 2 Tablespoons whole milk
- 2 tablespoons unsalted butter
- Smoked ham (8 slices)

Hollandaise sauce

- 4 egg yolks
- 1 tablespoon lemon juice
- Pinch cayenne
- Pinch salt
- 4 Tablespoons butter
- Pinch dry mustard

Yield: 4

Cooking Time: 30 minutes

Procedure:

Prepare the crepes batter first.

In a mixing bowl, combine the dry Ingredients: baking powder, flour, salt.

In a second bowl, combine the eggs, milk, sour cream, fresh herbs and stir.

Then, combine both mixtures in the biggest bowl.

Start making the hollandaise sauce next.

In a medium saucepan, combine the eggs yolks, lemon juice, butter and spices. Make sure you do stir constantly until you are satisfied with the consistency.

Start cooking the crepes one at a time in butter.

When assembling, add a few slices of ham in the crepe, fold and pour a generous portion of hollandaise sauce on top.

(22) Fruit and Pistachios Shake

No need to be scared, this green beverage is not all about green veggies. You can find a lot of green fruits and add some green nuts. But, I will be honest, I like to add spinach because it contains so much goodness, that is classed as a superfood.

List of Ingredients:

- 1 cup fresh baby spinach leaves
- 1 large Bartlett pear, peeled
- 1 Granny smith apple, peeled
- 1 cup soy milk
- 1 cup Greek plain yogurt
- 2 tablespoons pistachios
- ½ teaspoons vanilla extract

Yield: 2

Cooking Time: 10 minutes

MMMMMMMMMMMMMMMMMMMMMMMMMM

Procedure:

Another easy but great idea to prepare a quick healthy breakfast.

Peel and slice the apple and pear. Now, I usually keep the peels, but it is totally up to you.

Add the fruits in your high-speed blender container.

Add also the milk, yogurt and vanilla.

Place the pistachios in the food processor and activate for a minute, until it's powdery.

Then, also add the pistachios powder to the blender.

Activate until the mixture is very smooth.

Pour into 2 individual glasses and share with a loved one.

(23) Coffee Muffins

Coffee cakes and coffee muffins do go very well with a hot cup of coffee. However, you can enjoy a muffin with a glass of orange juice as well. Let's start by preparing these muffins, just the way we know how, with a lot of love and attention.

List of Ingredients:

- 1 tablespoon instant coffee
- 1 teaspoon baking powder
- Pinch cinnamon
- Pinch salt
- ½ cup brown sugar
- 1 cup coconut flour
- ¾ cup coconut milk
- 1/3 cup coconut oil (room temperature)
- 2 large eggs

Crumbly topping

- 1/3 cup brown sugar
- ½ cup rolled oats
- 1 teaspoon cinnamon
- 3 tablespoons unsalted butter
- 1 tablespoon whole milk or coconut milk

Yield: 8-12

Cooking Time: 50 minutes

MMMMMMMMMMMMMMMMMMMMMMMMM

Procedure:

Preheat the oven to 350degrees F.

Grease a muffin tin pan and set aside.

In a large mixing bowl, combine the coffee, baking powder, cinnamon, salt, brown sugar and coconut flour.

Add the eggs, coconut oil and gradually the coconut milk, while stirring.

Once the mixture is free of lumps, dump into the muffin tin holes.

Bake for 40 minutes.

Meanwhile, prepare the topping by mixing into a bowl all the listed ingredients.

After 20 minutes of muffins cooking, remove them briefly, add the topping and place back in the oven for another 20 minutes.

(24) Blueberries and French Toasts Casserole

Because I love French toast, I decided to make a casserole out of it. Also, every year, we organize a day as a family and go pick fresh blueberries, as there is nothing better than using ingredients you gather yourself. Let's see how we can combine both these wonderful ingredients into a yummy casserole.

List of Ingredients:

- 6 thick slices of bread (white or sourdough)
- 4 large eggs
- ¼ cup whole milk
- 2 cups fresh blueberries
- ½ cup sliced almonds
- ½ cup powdered sugar
- 1 tablespoon unsalted butter
- 2 cups cottage cheese, large curds
- Pinch cinnamon

Yield: 4-6

Cooking Time: 50 minutes

MMMMMMMMMMMMMMMMMMMMMMMMMM

Procedure:

Preheat the oven to 350 degrees F.

Grease large baking dish and set aside.

Proceed to prepare French toast as you normally would, but you will bake them instead of frying them.

In a mixing bowl, whisk the eggs with the milk, cinnamon.

Dip each slice of bread in it and set aside.

Mix the cottage cheese and the fresh blueberries together, along with the almonds.

This will be your bottom layer of the casserole.

Add the bread on top and spread some butter on it, as well as the powdered sugar.

Break in the oven for 30 minutes.

Serve in bowls.

(25) Avocado and Apple Salad

This salad will certainly catch your eye. It is as good as it looks, I promise you. I made this recipe often to bring at a breakfast potluck. People are impressed how well the avocado mixes with the apple and how pretty it looks when served.

List of Ingredients:

- 2 large sliced avocados
- 2 sliced apples (any kind you like)
- 2 Tablespoons lime juice
- 1 tablespoon lime zest
- 2 Tablespoons chopped sweet onion
- 3 Tablespoons olive oil
- 2 Tablespoons agave syrup
- ½ cup chopped walnuts

Yield: 4-6

Cooking Time: 30 minutes

MMMMMMMMMMMMMMMMMMMMMMMMMMMMM

Procedure:

Get all ingredients out and start peeled and slicing the avocados and apples.

Place in a large bowl, add the lime zest and lime juice.

Add also the agave syrup, olive oil and sweet onion.

Finally add the nuts and the smoked paprika.

Make sure you refrigerate until ready to serve.

About the Author

A native of Indianapolis, Indiana, Valeria Ray found her passion for cooking while she was studying English Literature at Oakland City University. She decided to try a cooking course with her friends and the experience changed her forever. She enrolled at the Art Institute of Indiana which offered extensive courses in the culinary Arts. Once Ray dipped her toe in the cooking world, she never looked back.

When Valeria graduated, she worked in French restaurants in the Indianapolis area until she became the head chef at one of the 5-star establishments in the area. Valeria's attention to taste and visual detail caught the eye of a local business person who expressed an interest in publishing her recipes. Valeria began her secondary career authoring cookbooks and e-books which she tackled with as much talent and gusto as her first career. Her passion for food leaps off the page of her books which have colourful anecdotes and stunning pictures of dishes she has prepared herself.

Valeria Ray lives in Indianapolis with her husband of 15 years, Tom, her daughter, Isobel and their loveable Golden Retriever, Goldy. Valeria enjoys cooking special dishes in her large, comfortable kitchen where the family gets involved in preparing meals. This successful, dynamic chef is an inspiration to culinary students and novice cooks everywhere.

Author's Afterthoughts

Thank you for Purchasing my book and taking the time to read it from front to back. I am always grateful when a reader chooses my work and I hope you enjoyed it!

With the vast selection available online, I am touched that you chose to be purchasing my work and take valuable time out of your life to read it. My hope is that you feel you made the right decision.

I very much would like to know what you thought of the book. Please take the time to write an honest and informative review on Amazon.com. Your experience and opinions will be of great benefit to me and those readers looking to make an informed choice.

With much thanks,

Valeria Ray

Printed in Great Britain
by Amazon